T0082450

Look at the Lights, My Love

ANNIE ERNAUX

Look at the Lights, My Love

*Translated from the French by
Alison L. Strayer*

A MARGELLOS
WORLD REPUBLIC OF LETTERS BOOK

Yale UNIVERSITY PRESS | NEW HAVEN & LONDON

The Margellos World Republic of Letters is dedicated to making literary works from around the globe available in English through translation. It brings to the English-speaking world the work of leading poets, novelists, essayists, philosophers, and playwrights from Europe, Latin America, Africa, Asia, and the Middle East to stimulate international discourse and creative exchange.

Originally published in France as *Regarde les lumières mon amour* by Éditions du Seuil.
Copyright © 2014 by Éditions du Seuil.
English translation copyright © 2023 by Yale University.

Yale University Press books may be purchased in quantity for educational, business, or promotional use. For information, please e-mail sales.press@yale.edu (US office) or sales@yaleup.co.uk (UK office).

Set in Source Serif type by Karen Stickler.
Printed in the United States of America.

Library of Congress Control Number: 2022950306
ISBN 978-0-300-26821-8 (pbk. : alk. paper)

A catalogue record for this book is available from the British Library.

This paper meets the requirements of ANSI/NISO Z39.48-1992 (Permanence of Paper).

10 9 8 7 6 5 4 3 2

The big supermarket down the road is always open:
all day its electric doors slide stolidly back and forth,
admitting and discharging streams of people. Its neon-lit
space is so impersonal and so eternal that it emanates both
comfort and alienation. Inside you can forget that you're
not alone, or that you are.

RACHEL CUSK, *Aftermath*

Look at the Lights, My Love

Twenty years ago, I found myself shopping in a superstore in Košice, Slovakia. It had just opened, the first in the city to appear after the fall of the communist regime. I don't know if that is how it got its name—Prior. At the entrance, a store employee authoritatively placed a basket in the hands of the—bewildered—customers. From a platform at least four meters high in the middle of the store, a woman supervised every movement of the people wandering from one department to another. Everything about their behavior signaled a lack of familiarity with self-service. They stood for a long time in front of items without touching them, or wavered, cautious, retraced their steps, irresolute, with the almost imperceptible faltering of bodies that have ventured into unknown territory. They were having their first experience of the superstore and its rules, displayed without subtlety by the management of Prior with the mandatory baskets and the warden on her elevated perch. I was troubled by this spectacle of a collective entry into consumerism, captured at the source.

I remembered the first time I entered a supermarket. It was in 1960, in the suburbs of London. The store was called, simply, Supermarket. The mother of the family for whom I worked as an au pair girl had sent me there with a shopping cart—which I did not like—and a list of food to buy. I have no precise memory of my thoughts and feelings. I know only that I felt a certain apprehension about going to a place that was alien to me, in terms of both its functioning and the language, of which I had a poor command. I quickly got into the habit of hanging around there with another French girl, also an au pair. We were enchanted and thrilled by the many kinds of yogurt—in our anorexic phase—and by the wide array of sweets—in our bulimic phase—and so granted ourselves the freedom to bolt down an entire pack of Smarties inside the store, without going through the checkout.

We choose our objects and our places of memory, or rather the spirit of the times decides what is worth remembering. Writers, artists, filmmakers play a role in the elaboration of this memory. Superstores, which over the past forty years in France the majority of people visit roughly fifty times a year, are only starting to be considered as places worthy of representation. Yet I realize, looking back in time, that for every period of my life I retain images of big-box superstores, with scenes, meetings, and people.

I remember:

the Carrefour on avenue de Genève in Annecy, where, in May 1968, we filled a shopping trolley (not yet a "cart") to the brim—because we feared a total lack of food supplies.

the Intermarché outside of La Charité-sur-Loire with its billboard reading "The Musketeers of Retail," a treat for the children after touring castles and churches in the summer, like the visits to the Leclerc in Osny after school, the same Leclerc where I would later meet former students whom I did not immediately recognize, and tears came to my eyes with the thought that I would never buy chocolate there again for my mother, who had just died.

the Major supermarket at the foot of the rock of Sancerre, the Continent on the heights of Rouen near the university, the Super-M in Cergy, chains whose disappearance underscores the melancholy of time.

the Mammouth store in Oiartzun, where we never did go, despite our desire to stock up on chorizo and turrón before the border (we were always too late), which became a family joke, a symbol of the contretemps and the inaccessible.

The superstore and supercenter cannot be reduced to their function in terms of *home economics,* to the "chore" of grocery shopping. They provoke thought, anchor sensation and emotion in memory. We could definitely write life narratives from the perspective of superstores visited on a regular basis. They are part of the landscape of childhood for everyone under fifty. Apart from a limited segment of the population—those who live in the center of Paris and the old historical cities— the superstore is a familiar space for all, whose regular use is part of daily life, but whose impact on our communities and our way of "building society" with our contemporaries in the twenty-first century we do not fully grasp. Yet when you think of it, there is no other space, public or private, where so many individuals so different in terms of age, income, education, geographic and ethnic background, and personal style, move about and rub shoulders with each other. No enclosed space where people are brought into greater contact with their fellow humans, dozens of times a year, and where each has a chance to catch a glimpse of others' ways of living and being. Politicians, journalists, "experts," all those who have never set foot in a superstore, do not know the social reality of France today.

I have, on numerous occasions, experienced the superstore as a great human meeting place, a spectacle—
the first time acutely and with a certain sense of shame.
In order to write, I had isolated myself off-season in a
village in the Nièvre, but I was unable to write. Going
"to Leclerc," five kilometers away, brought relief: by being among strangers, seeing people, I was "back in the
world" again. Back in the necessary presence of people.
And so discovering that I was the same as everyone who
drops by the shopping center for entertainment or escape from loneliness. Very spontaneously, I began to de-
scribe things seen in these supercenters.[1]

Therefore, in order to "relate life," ours today, I had
no hesitation about choosing superstores as my subject.
I saw an opportunity to provide an account of the real
practice of their routine use, far removed from conven-
tional discourses often tinged with aversion that these
so-called non-places arouse and which in no way corre-
spond to my experience of them.

So, from November 2012 to October 2013, I made a
record of most of my visits to the Auchan superstore in

1. *Journal du dehors* (Paris: Gallimard, 1993); *Exteriors,* trans. Tanya
Leslie (1996; London: Fitzcarraldo Editions, 2021), *La Vie extérieure*
(Paris: Gallimard, 2000); *Things Seen,* trans. Jonathan Kaplansky (Lin-
coln: University of Nebraska Press, 2010).

Cergy, where I usually go, for reasons of convenience and pleasure essentially linked to its location inside the Trois-Fontaines shopping center, the largest in Val-d'Oise. Accessible by foot from the RER train station, and by car directly from the A15 expressway, Trois-Fontaines is located at the heart of the Cergy-Préfecture district. All the public institutions are concentrated there—the prefecture, main post office, family allowance office, tax office, commuter train and bus terminals, credit union, police station, theater, media library, music conservatory, swimming pool, skating rink, etc., as well as several establishments of higher education (a faculty of literature, business school, a school of computer science, the National School of Art) and banks, such that I would readily define this space—which, incidentally, is called the *Grand Centre*—as a cluster or even a web of concentrated masses that together create considerable animation during the day and a desert landscape at night.

The shopping center occupies the greater part of this area. Imagine an enormous rectangular fortress of red-brown brick whose broad facade, the one facing the highway, is made of mirrored glass that reflects the clouds. The opposite facade, overlooking office buildings and a residential tower, is made entirely of brick, like an old factory in the North. Since its construction in 1972, a perpendicular wing has been added at one end, now primarily occupied by the FNAC store.[2] It is surrounded on three sides by huge, multilevel parking garages, half of which are covered. Ten porticoes give access to the inside; several monumental ones remind you of a temple entrance, half-Greek, half-Asian, with their four columns crowned by two distant roofs in the shape of an arc, the top one made of glass and metal, gracefully extending over all that lies below.

Trois-Fontaines is a new kind of town center. Owned by a private group, it is completely closed and monitored: no one can enter, outside of set hours. When you walk by it late at night, after getting off the commuter train, its silent mass is more desolate than a cemetery.

Here, existing together on three levels, are all the shops and payable services that a given population is likely to need: a supercenter, fashion boutiques, hair salons, a medical center and pharmacies, a daycare center, fast food restaurants, cigarette-magazine-newspaper vendors, etc. There are free restrooms, and wheelchairs on loan. But the only café, Le Troquet, the Tritons movie theater, and Le Temps de Vivre bookstore have disappeared. Only a few high-end brands can be found. The customers, for the most part, belong to the middle and working classes.

2. French chain specializing in cultural products (music, literature, movies, video games) and electronics (computers, TVs).

For those not used to it, the place is disorienting—not as a labyrinth is, like the city of Venice, but as a result of a geometric structure in which shops that are easily confused with one another are aligned on either side of a right-angled walkway. This is a vertigo produced by symmetry, reinforced by the fact that the space is enclosed, though open to the daylight through a big glass canopy that replaces the roof.

The Auchan superstore occupies almost half of the center's surface area, on two levels. It is the heart of the shopping center, supplying all the other businesses with a flow of customers. Its supremacy is plain to see on the pediment over the center's main entrance, where its name is written in huge sprawling letters, eclipsing the ones in smaller print for FNAC and Darty.[3] The covered shopping-cart corrals in the parking garages bear the same logo, red with a bird. It is the store with the longest opening hours, from 8:30 a.m. to 10 p.m., while the others are open only from 10 a.m. to 8 p.m. Inside the center, the Auchan superstore is a self-contained enclave that, in addition to food, sells household appliances, clothing, books, and newspapers, and offers ser-

3. French electrical appliance store. It was bought by FNAC in 2016.

vices such as ticketing, travel, photo processing, etc. In a sense, it replicates the goods and services that may be obtained from other businesses, such as Darty, that is, when it has not driven them out of the center, where there are no more bakeries, butcher shops, wine merchants, etc. Level 1, non-food items, is in the shape of a long rectangle. It is linked by escalator to Level 2, whose surface is divided into two spaces, connected but set at right angles to each other, which, by reducing the infinite horizon of merchandise, mitigates the impression of immensity. All entrances are patrolled by security guards.

That's it for the physiognomy of the premises, through which I roamed as usual, shopping list in hand, but trying to pay closer attention than I ordinarily would to all its actors, the employees and customers, as well as the business strategies. Therefore, not a systematic investigation or exploration but a journal, the form most in keeping with my temperament, which is partial to the impressionistic recording of things, people, and atmospheres. A free statement of observations and sensations, aimed at capturing something of the life of the place.

2012

THURSDAY, NOVEMBER 8

It is cold and gray. Felt a sort of rush of pleasure earlier at the idea of going to Trois-Fontaines and doing some necessary shopping at Auchan. As a way of breaking up the writing day, an effortless distraction in a familiar place.

Once you have gone through the boom gates giving access (for a fee) to the car park, you may be faced with a series of pitfalls that make the shopping trip frustrating from the get-go: having to drive around a long time before finding a spot that is not to hell and gone, far from an entrance; realizing that you don't have a euro coin with which to unlock a cart, or that the cart that you've taken not only veers to one side, irrepressibly, but also contains rubbish from the previous user. Yet to come upon an empty spot right away, or a spot that someone is just leaving and is very close to your favorite entrance, is a good omen. Another is to find yourself a clean and easily maneuvered shopping cart. I'm lucky on both counts today.

Lots of people in the concourse of the center—it is still the All Saints holiday period—but fewer in Auchan. Halloween having come and gone, the scene is set for Christmas. At the entrance is a huge scaffolding, made of decorated bottles—CHAMPAGNE AT 6.31 EUROS PER BOTTLE, 20% OFF WITH THE AUCHAN CARD (no mention of the brand). Boxes of chocolates. Decorations for the table and the tree. Yellow signs as far as the eye can see, with PROMO in huge black letters. But there are few shoppers on this level, as if people were resisting commercial time, waiting for the right moment or (more likely) their paycheck at the end of the month.

The toys occupy several rows of shelves, rigorously separated into "Boys" and "Girls." For the former, there are feats of daring—Spiderman—outer space, sound and fury—cars, planes, tanks, robots, punching bags—all in different shades of violent red, green, and yellow. For the others, there is the indoor world, housecleaning, seduction, and playing mother and baby. "My mini-mart," "My housekeeping supplies," "My mini-cooking set," "My iron," "My baby care starter kit." A transparent "food bag" is hideously filled with what looks to be a mixture of turds and vomit—croissants and other plastic foods. Seeing a doctor's kit in the midst of all the domestic paraphernalia is a relief, almost. Gender-role conditioning does not bother with subtlety or imagination: it's all "just like mom" in miniature. Across the aisle: the candy colors of cosmetic bags, dressing tables with a mirror and seat, for putting on one's face; Snow White and princess costumes. Further on, shelves thirty-feet high, covered with dolls from top to bottom. An ad for a Barbie driving a Volkswagen, 29.90€. I am shaken with anger and a feeling of powerlessness. I think of Femen:[4] this is where you have to come, to places where our unconscious minds are shaped, and slash and burn all these objects of transmission. I'll be there.

A little further still, in the bookstore area, a lone customer—an older lady—wanders from one table to another. Every time I venture in there, I leave sad and discouraged. It's not because they don't have my books— they do, a few in the "Pocket" section—but, with only a few exceptions, the selection obeys a single criterion, that of sales. The bestsellers are displayed over an area about ten feet wide, numbered from one to ten, in huge figures, as at the horse races at Longchamp. Anything that can be designated "literature" occupies the smallest part of this space dedicated to practical topics, games, travel, religion, etc.

4. Radical feminist activist group started in Ukraine in 2008. By 2014, the year this book was published, Femen had its largest membership in France. The organization became internationally known for organizing controversial topless protests.

I notice a sign overhead: OUT OF RESPECT FOR OUR CUSTOMERS, IT IS FORBIDDEN TO READ THE MAGAZINES IN THE STORE. THANK YOU FOR YOUR UNDERSTANDING.

What irritates me the most about this prohibition is the use of the possessive "our," instead of the "the" one would expect. Neither I nor the others are the property of Auchan, and we are even less its partners: its customers are not mine, not ours. This "our" is phony and ingratiating.

Upstairs, on the food level, there are lots of people. The school holiday atmosphere is palpable. There is a carefree, out-for-a-stroll feeling in the air. Many have no shopping cart or basket. Teenagers roam back and forth across the central aisle of circulation, perpendicular to the rows of shelves. They hang about, flit between the shopping carts of elderly couples, and of women besieged by children who amuse themselves by running away, coming back, and running away again. A girl removes the headphones paired with her cell phone to answer her mother. Another girl, in the mineral-water zone at the very back, talks on the phone, resting her head against a pack of Evian: "Did you get permission to take photos or not?" It is possible to isolate oneself and carry on a conversation in a superstore as serenely as in a garden.

The floor-cleaning machine, driven by a blonde woman, fiftyish, wearing a blue uniform, is having trouble making its way through all the people. This delicate job of driver, which has something majestic about it— she looms over the customers from her elevated seat— seems to me, perhaps wrongly, more rewarding than that of an employee assigned to stock shelves.

Other store employees—salespeople, department managers, pallet handlers, etc.—all wear the same uniform: a sleeveless black jacket, vaguely Mao style, with AUCHAN printed on it in big white letters. I see one chatting in a familiar way with an Asian customer whose shopping cart contains only four large bags of plain rice. I realize that I don't know anyone who works here.

Until now, I have always refused to get the Auchan customer loyalty card. To the question ritually asked at the checkout, "Do you have a loyalty card?," I usually reply, just as ritualistically, "I am loyal to no one!" This is quite an exaggeration, but I simply do not want to submit to the consumerist inducement strategy practiced by all mass merchandisers. Today I said, "How do you get one?," curious as to what information I would be required to provide. None, to my surprise. The cashier immediately hands me a card with the Auchan logo and a barcode on the back. There is no quicker and more discreet way to link customers to a brand, through the rewards program whereby one rakes in euros' worth of savings by obeying the prescription to buy such-and-such an item.

MONDAY, NOVEMBER 12

Afternoon. At the entrance to Auchan, for today's small shopping trip, I took only a wheeled basket, made of red plastic, deep and very maneuverable.

I walk past the near-deserted fishmonger's stall. There's a strong odor, unavoidable in spite of the ice, due to the heat pervading the entire store. On the right side of the stall is an impressive layer of overlapping salt cod fillets, which resemble a sort of sloped roof with old grayish tiles. On the floor is a stack of closed crates, full of cod: 65€ for 10 kg. A black woman in a long, floral-print dress stops in front of them, hesitates, walks away.

[Dilemma. Am I going to write "a black woman"—or "an African woman," though I'm not sure she is African—or simply "a woman"? I am faced with a choice, which will influence the way in which this journal will be read, especially today. To write "a woman" is to erase a physical characteristic I can't not have immediately seen. In short it is, implicitly, to "whiten" this woman because the white reader will, instinctively, imagine a white woman. It is to deny a part of her being, and not the least of them, her skin. Textually deny her visibility. Exactly the opposite of what I want and am committed to doing in my writing: to give people, here in this journal, the same presence and space they occupy in the life of the superstore. Not to write a manifesto in favor of ethnic diversity, but simply give those who frequent the same space as me the existence and visibility to which they are entitled. So I will write "a black woman," "an Asian man," "Arab teenagers" whenever it suits me.]

Fruits and vegetables. An island of loose Italia grapes in bulk. Many people pick out one or two and eat them, more or less discreetly, with a sort of collective sense of permission whereby individuals limit themselves to a few grapes and are further kept in check by others' eyes upon them. To do the same with apples or pears would overstep the boundaries of this unspoken right. And indeed, I am "at the apples" now. An employee is unloading crates. I ask him if he has russet apples. The few that remain in the stall are looking worse for wear.

"I'm putting some out just for you!" He sets down a full crate in front of me. "Are they for pies? I do them in the oven, I prefer them oven-baked."

"I do them in the microwave, ten minutes is enough."

He teaches me how to use the new electronic scale.

He is talkative. I am old enough and he is young enough for this exchange to be something other than mere civility. I would like to ask him about his salary. I don't dare. I am unable to step outside my status of customer.

Suddenly there's a man walking up and down a spacious aisle, swaying slightly, with an open can of Red Bull in his hand. Nothing else—no basket or shopping cart. The other hand is in the back pocket of his jeans, which are falling off him a little. A knit cap is pulled down over his head. I am starting to be afraid for him because of the surveillance cameras—I haven't yet figured out where they are—and the security guards. Among the regular clientele of this Auchan, which every year has grown more ethnically diverse, homeless people, the tipsy kind, have disappeared. A kind of "normal consumer" now prevails, either because the others have been refused entry by security guards or through self-exclusion.

At the automatic checkout, I wait behind a guy with a ponytail, a long black leather coat, and Doc Martens. This type of checkout, reserved for "ten items or less," is mainly used by the young; few are over fifty. I suspect that for many the self-checkout seems complicated, though an employee is posted a few steps away to provide assistance. A machine becomes available. Once again, it takes me a lot of time to perform the various maneuvers. As I am putting my items into a plastic bag, for which you pay three centimes, I realize that a second bag is clinging to it, unaccounted for by the machine. Involuntarily I have cheated. I wonder afterward if the self-checkout register is capable of detecting a barcode that has been replaced by another, or any other kind of crafty scheme. This kind of device induces moral indifference. With a machine, we do not feel we are stealing.

FRIDAY, NOVEMBER 16

5 p.m. I head for the Auchan pharmacy, located within the superstore, not far from the other health and beauty products, but self-contained, with its own checkout and a saleswoman capable of advising. The aisles are so narrow that shopping carts must be left at the entrance. A sign: FRIDAY—BUY 2 GET 30% OFF. Due to the predictable increase in the number of customers, mostly women, rarely men, an additional saleswoman is on duty, self-confident, edgy, probably a grade above the usual saleswoman (her position of authority shows in her face and gestures). A group of girls enter, white

and black, including a young mother with a child in a stroller. They crowd around the makeup counter and confer in animated murmurs, heads pressed together. A middle-aged Eurasian woman hovers in front of the diet foods, and ends up taking a batch of two packs of Milical cookies on sale.

The pharmacy—like some organic food aisles—requires long periods of standing. People fall into a meditative state before the products designed to restore the waistline, bowel movements and sleep, designed to help one live better, be better. These are the shelves of dreams and desires, of hope—therapy shelves, in a sense; but the best part comes before the item is placed in the cart.

Though I have no plans to buy any, the toys have a magnetic appeal for me, as they do, perhaps, for the three young people, twentyish, who are wandering through the section. They stop in front of the masks. One of them lightly touches the transparent plastic lid of a robot costume and they all start reminiscing with excitement—"I had one like that!" They look happy, lovably childish.

A young woman slowly passes through the doll aisle. The little girl of six or eight behind her is calling out for I-don't-know-which doll. Her mother pulls her away saying "Come on, you'll be getting one from Green Santa."

Green Santa is the one from the Secours Populaire[5] who distributes toys to the children of poor parents.

There is a line at the fishmonger's, sign of a general integration of the Catholic tradition. In fact, the only belief that leads people to buy fish on Fridays is that it's fresher than on other days.

Not far, posted here and there above the bins of fresh meat, are signs reading: FRESH MEAT AT UNDER 1 EURO; BUDGET-FRIENDLY OPTIONS FROM AUCHAN; MEAT AT 1 EURO PER PERSON.

The language of seduction, humanitarian style. The superstore calculates the cost of the ration on the plate. But what is the weight? Didn't see; it's probably there in very fine print.

Near the "International" aisles, followed by the halal and kosher sections, is a corner of the store where no one dares to go, a kind of gourmet grocery store, a Bon Marché food emporium in miniature. Pretentious section headings—Oil Cellar, Pasta Cellar. A 330 ml bottle of L'Olivier oil costs 14€, and all the rest is correspondingly overpriced, spices, biscuits and canned goods with brand names such as Albert Ménès, Table de Mathilde.

5. Secours Populaire Français, or French Popular Relief, is a French nonprofit organization founded in 1945, dedicated to fighting poverty and discrimination in public life.

Does this special reserve, always deserted, enhance Auchan's status? It is here I saw a handsome mouse dart out from under the aisle of jams and preserves one day. Rodents evade the surveillance cameras far more easily than we do.

As there are many more very poor than very rich people, the everyday deals section occupies an area five times larger than the one for gourmet foods. Until 2007, it was located near the organic section, small at the time, where the two wings of Level 2 intersect, so that people crossed it on their way from one wing to the other. Management probably judged it more cost-effective to extend and multiply the shelves of (expensive) organic products in this strategic space, and moved the everyday deals section to an enclave at the very back of the second floor, which it shares with pet supplies. That way, it is less of a blot on the landscape than if it were located right in the middle of the store. If you don't have a dog or cat, you can very easily ignore its existence. It is the provisioning site for *cheap eaters,* an expression coined by Thomas Bernhard, and everything about the place confirms it. To the same degree as cat and dog food with its colorful packaging is presented as delicious and joy-inducing, the discount food for people, in the section just beside it, could not be less attractive, with items stacked on pallets on the floor or in wooden crates on shelving.

Even the refrigerated displays look bad. Everything is in large quantities, eggs in cartons of 30, *pain au chocolat* in packs of 14 for 1.89€. No brand names, only the contents, written in big letters: "Brussels sprouts," "Pastries," "Chocolate pound cake"—or obscure brands, premium coffee, ratatouille. The labels extol the quality of products that wholly lack it: "premium" oil.

Across from it is the bulk section, containing bins full of all kinds of things, sweets and cocktail snacks that one stuffs in a bag and weighs.

Here, the usual language of seduction, made up of false benevolence and promised happiness, is replaced by the language of explicit threats. For the entire length of the bulk section, a sign in red letters warns: CONSUMPTION ON THE PREMISES PROHIBITED, and another, higher up, more courteous, reads:

CONSUMPTION ON THE PREMISES IS
    PROHIBITED.
THANK YOU FOR YOUR UNDERSTANDING.
LIFE. REAL LIFE. AUCHAN.

A sign above the scales preempts the temptation to cheat: DEAR CUSTOMERS, WE INFORM YOU THAT THE NAME AND WEIGHT OF YOUR ITEMS MAY BE MONITORED AT THE CHECKOUT. A warning meant for a population presumed dangerous, since it does not appear above the scales in the fruit and vegetable area in the "normal" part of the store.

A woman appears with a little red-haired boy next to a stroller. He makes a dash for the candies. "Sammy! Sammy!" the mother cries. He has already plunged his hand into a bin and triumphantly brings her a handful of sweets. I smile at the scene. Not the mother, who avoids my eyes.

At the checkout, an argument between a grandmother and her granddaughter of about six or eight.

"Do you want the Kiki or the perfume? Which do you prefer? [It seems the perfume is already in the basket.] You can't have everything in life. Do you think Grandma has everything she wants? The same goes for you."

"I want the Kiki."

The grandmother removes the perfume, marked Walt Disney, from the basket and drops it on a nearby gondola display while the little girl goes to get the Kiki. She comes back with it tightly clasped in her hand. It's a little monkey. Surreptitiously, with a hurried gesture, the grandmother retrieves the perfume. Without a word she throws it back in the shopping basket, a disgruntled look on her face. She knows that it is wrong of her to act in this way, but she cannot refrain from doing so. From wanting to make her granddaughter happy. From loving to be loved by her. In the world of the superstore and the free-market economy, loving children means buying them as many things as possible.

TUESDAY, NOVEMBER 20

For a long time I did not know that Auchan belonged to a family, the Mulliezes, who also own Leroy Merlin, Kiloutou, Decathlon, Midas, Flunch, Jules, etc. I don't imagine that many of the people here today are aware of it. I wonder what knowing it has changed for me. They are shadows, mythical beings. In Annecy, it was once rumored that the Fournier family—creator of the first Carrefour in that city—ate from golden dishes.

SATURDAY, NOVEMBER 24

I arrive at Trois-Fontaines in the early afternoon. Congestion in the parking garage. The moment I walk into the center, I am struck by the difference in clientele compared to other days. There are more couples and families, often with small children, more women with headscarves. A very tangible atmosphere of excitement and expenditure (or desire to spend), multiplied by the number of individuals. Something like a Great Refueling. Shopping carts are overflowing.

The "magic of Christmas" is evident everywhere. Garlands ripple down like silver rain above the escalators and walls. The center never looks more like a flamboyant Gothic cathedral than at this time of year. At the entrance to Auchan, gray-haired ladies with the look of charity volunteers distribute transparent bags. It is National Food Bank day. One of the ladies hands me a flyer showing the products to be bought, preferably canned goods, sugar, coffee, oil. She tells me that hygiene items and baby food are also needed. Then, softly: "No pasta, please, last year we had three tons of it!" Ah! Filthy rotten donors! All right, then, no penny-pinching kindness. And a bit of imagination, please! The discomfort and conundrum of charity. I make it a point of honor to forgo the cheapest products and buy "as if for myself." I have the cheerful feeling that taking time to choose Blédina chicken with green vegetables and Rik & Rok chocolate is more honorable than giving money. Healthy charity. [Later, at the checkout, when I empty the contents of the transparent bag onto the conveyor belt, it seems to me there is a good fifty euros' worth of food. But on checking, I see I have overestimated the value of my gesture: only twenty-eight euros.]

In the cheese department, I notice a young couple. They waver. As if they were in an unfamiliar situation, as if this were new to them. Buying groceries as a couple for the first time confirms that a shared life is truly beginning. It means making adjustments for budgets and tastes, united around the basic need to eat. Proposing that a man or woman accompany you to the superstore is a world away from inviting them to the movies, or to the café for a drink. There is no seductive swagger, no possibility of cheating. Do you like Roquefort? Reblochon? That one is straight from the farm. Why don't we make roast chicken?

The toy section is less crowded than expected. A couple of grandparents gaze anxiously at a large doll, as if her red lips and fixed stare were about to emit a sign that it is she and not another they must choose. A man drags his kid away from the remote-controlled cars, "Come on, let's go find *mumma*." I heard and said *mumma* throughout my childhood, not *mom*. The man who just reminded me of this is from Africa or the West Indies.

People constantly refer to weekend grocery shopping as a "chore." Lack of awareness or bad faith? It could be considered the price of prosperity, labor born of affluence. Subsistence has always required labor, much more so in the past than today, except for the privileged, who had servants to take care of it.

This afternoon, people are clearly taking their time.

At the exit, flat boxes are spread over the ground. The food bank ladies dispatch the items people have given them, oil here, coffee there, etc. The stark impression of a market for the poor, exposed in broad daylight.

WEDNESDAY, NOVEMBER 28

A textile factory in Bangladesh was destroyed by fire, and 112 people died, mostly women, who worked for a salary of 29.50€ per month. The building had nine floors; it should not have had more than three. The workers were trapped inside, unable to escape.

This factory, Tazreen, made polo tops, T-shirts, etc. for Auchan, Carrefour, Pimkie, Go Sport, Cora, C&A, H&M.

Of course, crocodile tears aside, we who blithely reap the benefits of that slave labor cannot be counted on to change anything at all. Revolution will come only from the exploited themselves, on the other side of the world. Even the unemployed French, victims of corporate relocations, are happy enough to be able to buy themselves a T-shirt for seven euros.

THURSDAY, NOVEMBER 29

An anomaly in a food aisle at Auchan: an elegant girl in a short-sleeved dress, pulling a wheeled suitcase. No doubt she's just got off the RER and is taking advantage of the shopping center's proximity to do a few errands.

Here, more than anywhere else, I have trouble discerning and comprehending the present moment, the meaning of everything that I see while moving about. All I see of people is their bodies, their appearance, their gestures. And what they put in their basket or cart. From which I deduce their standard of living, more or less. But I cannot see the essential, which remains concealed even by the overflowing carts of weekend shopping: the incessant calculations most people are forced to do, back and forth, between the need to eat and the price of food. The less money one has, the more carefully one must shop, making no mistakes. More time is needed. A list must be made. The best deals in the sales flyer must be selected. This is a form of economic labor, uncounted and obsessive, that fully occupies thousands of women and men. The beginning of wealth, of the levity of wealth, is discernible in the act of taking an item from a shelf of food without first checking the price. The humiliation inflicted by commercial goods: they are too expensive, so I'm worth nothing.

On Level 2, if one wants to sit down, there is a grand total of two small plastic chairs in the corridor between the two wings, next to a water fountain. The superstore is designed for efficient circulation. Seating would hamper this and encourage rest. Clearly, consumer venues are designed like workplaces: fewer breaks for optimal return. The chairs are very often occupied by middle-aged women holding a grocery cart in front of them by the handle, or by mothers with children to whom they are giving food or drink.

In the bookshop area there is just one man, leafing through *The Secret Lives of Great Historical Figures.* Displayed side by side are *The Holy Quran, The Quran for Dummies, The Bible for Dummies.* Maybe it is only in superstores that you can find these books and leaf through them with no fear of being watched.

People take photos everywhere, all the time. But inside Auchan, I've never seen anyone taking photos with a cell phone. Is it allowed?

WEDNESDAY, DECEMBER 5

4 p.m. Rain. Inside the shopping center, we don't see the weather. The space bears no sign of it. It cannot be detected anywhere. Shops are replaced, shelves are ro-

tated, items refreshed. The renewal changes nothing, fundamentally, and always follows the same cycle, from January sales to the year-end holidays, through the big summer sales and back to school.

At this time, to walk through one of the doors of the shopping center is to abruptly land in the effervescence, trepidation, and sparkle of things, an entire world one would never guess was there while standing in the cold of the parking lot in front of this red-brick Kremlin.

Lots of people in the toy section at Auchan today. Lots of children. Rigorously separated. No girls in front of the Spiderman cars and costumes, no boys in front of the Barbies, Hello Kitty, the Rik & Rok dolls that cry.

Once, my two-year-old son wanted a doll. His parents felt that his interest in the opposite sex grew out of a legitimate desire and curiosity, and he got the doll.

In the big designated space for phones and computers—ELECTRONICS—a majority of male customers, and the sales personnel are all men: young, generally personable, moving between counters in a laid-back manner, conscious of their expertise. At a glance, you'd think they were an aristocracy, the kind who never miss a chance to assume a patronizing attitude toward customers, especially female ones. Indeed, two women are inquiring about a cell phone for a little girl, "something

simple, just to get home from school," which makes the
two guys at the stand laugh and crack jokes. I need a USB
key. I am acutely aware that to ask the salesman to rouse
himself and explain how many gigabytes I need mani-
fests gross ignorance, a fact to which his faint smile at-
tests. This is a predominantly male department. Also the
one with the greatest number of salesmen, who often
stand around with nothing to do. There are no salespeople at all in the bookstore.

It is impossible to access Level 2 without seeing the
fishmonger's counter at the top of the escalator. There
is conger eel, rock salmon at 6.99€ per kilo, mussels at
2.99, monkfish tail at 14.95. Prices are in gigantic letters,
always on the same acid yellow background. I am aware
that this kind of excess functions as a kind of hypno-
sis—I'm being led to believe that these fish are literally
being *given away*. The employees move around quickly,
wearing boots, blue aprons, and caps. The man who I
think is in charge—young face, gray hair under the cap—
scoops ice in large handfuls from a bin and throws it
onto the stall. He tells another employee how to arrange
the sea bass parallel to each other before sprinkling a
thin layer of ice on top. He asks me what I would like.
"Nothing, I'm looking at you."

"Oh?"

"I'm writing about superstores."

Suddenly he is interested. I ask how long he's been working at Auchan. "Twenty years!" he says with the kind of pride that comes from things that endure, no matter what they are—a job, a marriage, even a life, etc. He says, "I've been at the fishmonger's here for eleven!" Pride most of all about his work, no longer that of a subordinate but of a person in charge at every level, in the selection, preparation, and sale of a fragile food item. At no time during our conversation does he lose sight of his stall. A customer arrives. He leaves me right away, apologizing.

Because of his expertise, he, along with the butcher, the baker, and the cheesemonger, enjoys an autonomy and a responsibility that set him apart. Before being Auchan employees, they were all *craftspeople,* artisans. They form a kind of nobility, generally male.

Too many people at the regular checkouts. Reluctantly I head for the self-checkout, reserved for a maximum of ten items. Ahead of me is a lone man, fiftyish, with a slice of pizza at 1.75, a baguette in cellophane, bananas, and tangerines. Behind me are students reminiscing about their high school. One holds a tub of Häagen-Dazs ice cream. One of the self-checkout machines is out of order, which is often the case. I am relieved that the one that falls to me is farthest from the line and the anxious eyes of the other customers, who assess their chances of getting through quickly on the basis of the skill or ineptitude of the person ahead. The perversity of the self-checkout system: the irritation aroused by a slower cashier is now transferred to the customer.

In fact, it is a stressful, terror-inducing system, in which you must follow instructions to the letter if you are to succeed in taking the merchandise home. This operation is divided into phases whose order cannot possibly be disrupted, otherwise the bossy computer-generated voice repeats "Place the item on the scale, scan the barcode," as many times as required, creating the impression that the machine is growing increasingly annoyed and considers you useless and incompetent. Today, not having had to endure any reprimands from the voice, I feel, with an A-student's vanity, as if I've just scored 10/10.

The growing certainty that consumer docility knows no bounds.

FRIDAY, DECEMBER 7

8:45 p.m. In the shopping center, all the stores have been closed for three-quarters of an hour. Some, like the pharmacy, have lowered an iron shutter. Other dimly lit storefronts are covered with a kind of metallic mesh through which it is possible to glimpse displays in subdued lighting. Some of the Christmas lights have been extinguished, and the passages between stores are in semi-darkness. The people I pass look ghostly. There is a feeling of desolation, more than on other nights when I go late to Auchan, the only business still open other than McDonald's and Flunch. Wonderland has been switched off until morning. I think of a disturbing short story by Jon Raymond, "Young Bodies," in which a girl and a boy find themselves locked overnight in a store in a shopping center, unable to escape without setting off the alarm.

All the light has fled to the superstore, which is fairly empty. In the personal care section, the saleswoman packs my shampoo and takes payment without interrupting her phone conversation. In the evening, near closing time, the attitude of the staff conveys a kind of permission to unwind, a weary slowness.

The shelves are in shambles. Full of holes. There is no more icing sugar. Pallets are half empty. There's a feeling of arriving at the banquet after the guests have gone home.

As usual, I notice a contrast between the nighttime customers, younger and more ethnically diverse, and those of daytime. Whole segments of the clientele are segregated from each other by the hours during which they do their shopping. Early morning is the time for retired couples, unhurried and well organized, with their own shopping bags and their checkbooks, from which they will carefully detach a check at the cash register, remembering to record the amount on the stub.

In the mid-afternoon, there are many women on their own—middle-aged, or young with children—who shop with their own grocery carts made of wipe-clean fabric, a sign that they came on foot or by bus, because they don't know how to drive, or because they don't own a car.

At 5 p.m., the after-work crowd starts pouring in. The pace grows brisker, more jarring. Schoolchildren with mothers. High-school students. Between 8 and 10 p.m., university students and—more rare at other times of day—women in long dresses and headscarves, always accompanied by a man. Do these couples choose the evening for reasons of convenience, or because at this later, off-peak hour they feel less as if they're being *stared at?*

There are people, entire segments of the clientele, who will never meet.

The local newspaper informs me that the Cergy region is home to 130 different nationalities. There is no place where they are more often in each other's company than at Trois-Fontaines, at Auchan. It is there that we get used to being in close proximity to each other, driven by the same essential need to feed and clothe ourselves. Whether we like it or not, here we form a community of desires.

Over the past fifteen years, it has not been the presence of "visible minorities" that I notice in a given place, but their absence.

WEDNESDAY, DECEMBER 12

The parking garage at the center started charging a fee fifteen years ago because train commuters were leaving their vehicles there all day, preventing customers from parking. Still, as one is reminded at every turn, the first two-and-a-half hours are free. Entry is generally uneventful—press a button and the machine delivers a ticket—but departure is sometimes more difficult because the free parking limit has been exceeded, or the system has unexpectedly shut down, for which we readily blame the first motorist caught overstaying his free time. To avoid paying, some freeloaders pull up close to the car ahead when the gate lifts (the same goes for some truckers at tollbooths on the highway). Late at night, it is not unusual to find the exit barriers open, perhaps to prevent them from being deliberately rammed.

The men and women who approached me earlier in the parking garage to ask me for a euro have disappeared. There are more and more homeless people in society as a whole, but fewer and fewer around the shopping center, except in two areas that are not part of the center's private territory:

near the shady entrance, in a recess between the blind wall behind which Auchan is located and the Caisse d'Epargne building, partially transformed into a university library. And indeed, the low wall by the library is where they sit when the sun comes out, watching people pass—and many do go by at this part of the concrete slab that connects the Préfecture, RER station, bus depot, post office, etc. to the shopping center;

in front of the entrance that leads to a busy pedestrian street, lined with independent shops and partly covered by arcades that offer good shelter. This is the zone for panhandling and also for gathering signatures for more or less credible causes, inevitably accompanied by a request for a donation.

In the center, there are several flights of escalators going up and down between levels, including an inclined moving walkway that allows for access with a shopping cart. There are more inside the superstore, connecting the two levels: two going up, but only one going down. In these moments when we are forced to stand still, one behind the other, glances are exchanged between the people going up and those going down. We can peer at one another with frank curiosity, like the passengers of two trains moving slowly through a station in opposite directions.

In what way are we present to each other?

At times, here, I feel like a smooth surface reflecting other people and the signs hanging over their heads.

TUESDAY, DECEMBER 18

Afternoon. A dense crowd as soon as one enters the shopping center. A very loud buzzing noise through which the music can barely be heard. On the inclined moving walkway, under the glass roof, we ascend toward the lights and garlands hanging down like necklaces of precious stones. The young woman in front of me with a little girl in a stroller looks up and smiles. She leans down toward the child. "Look at the lights, my love!"

Coming out of Auchan is a very old man, very stooped, in a baggy overcoat. He moves along slowly with a cane, shuffling in his ragged shoes. His head droops over his chest and I see only his neck. In his free hand, he carries an ancient shopping bag. I am moved. He is like an admirable sort of beetle, come to brave the dangers of an unknown territory to bring home food.

2013

MONDAY, JANUARY 7

Dolls and toys piled pell-mell in a large fabric bin, 50 percent off. There could be no clearer demonstration of their function: *pure symbols* of the festive season. The season having ended, Barbies and Hello Kittys have remained exactly the same but simply lost their festive value. No one is rooting around in this rubbish bin of new toys. Yet one could find a doll or a costume in there, at a lower price, for a birthday gift or even next year's Christmas. The downgrading of a toy to a piece of scrap is repugnant. Mass retail rules our desires. On today's program of longed-for items are traditional *galette des rois* and household linens, from duvet covers to tea towels.

There are people, often none too young, who talk to themselves in front of the shelves, conversing out loud with the merchandise. Expressing their opinion or dissatisfaction, knowing they can be heard by customers nearby. It is better to be heard. A little woman gazing at the tins of sardines turns to me and laughs: "Sardines with hot peppers are not for me!" I smile back at her. A vague way of signaling agreement with her reasons for caution but also my intention to leave it at that. Called as witness to her life, I hide. Yet these yearnings for communication expressed by strangers inexplicably move me.

I take advantage of the dearth of customers in the everyday deals section to photograph the prohibition signs with my mobile phone. I've barely had time to take one when a man appears at my side. According to his badge, he's from Security.

"You're not allowed to take photos in the store, it is forbidden."

"Why?"

"It's forbidden. Those are the rules."

"I'm doing a reportage."

"Then you have to ask for permission from management."

I won't do anything. I want to stay in my usual role, that of a customer, and not draw attention to my presence.

TUESDAY, JANUARY 22

In the deserted automotive accessories department, a small black child played with a large cardboard box in the aisle. I wanted to photograph him. Then I wondered if there was not something of the colonial picturesque in my desire.

The curious impression that time here does not move but is a constantly cycling present, that there is no History here. Even my memory is mute. It's only when I'm away from here, writing it all down at home, that I recall scenes I've seen elsewhere, in other superstores and other times.

Carrefour, Annecy. The early 1970s. A winter evening, in the liquor section. Two or three guys facing a girl who is all alone. One sneers, "I'm telling you, it can't be mine!" and the others laugh. Not her, red-faced and serious, confronted with this bold public denial of paternity, to her great misfortune, since legal abortion did not exist then. That day, for the first time, it occurred to me that the graceless hangar was full of stories, lives. I wondered why superstores never appeared in the novels that were published, and how much time was required for a new reality to achieve literary dignity.

Today's hypotheses:

1) the supermarket is linked to subsistence, the business of women, who have long been its main users. And that which falls within the domain of activities more or less specific to women is traditionally invisible, does not count—like the domestic work they perform, moreover. That which has no value in life has none in literature.

2) until the 1970s, writers, women and men combined, were mostly from bourgeois backgrounds and lived in Paris, where superstores did not yet exist. (I don't see Alain Robbe-Grillet, Nathalie Sarraute, or Françoise Sagan doing their shopping in a superstore; Georges Perec yes, but I may be wrong about that.)

MONDAY, FEBRUARY 4

In June 1978, I spent a month alone in the country. The day of my return to Cergy, upon seeing that the cupboards and fridge were empty, I rushed out to Trois-Fontaines. The moment I passed through Gate 6, I thought with astonishment that I'd missed the place, and to be back there gave me a strange feeling of satisfaction. It was like an extension of my private universe of which I'd been deprived without my knowing.

I've often fled to the shopping center to forget the dis-
satisfactions of writing, losing myself in the crowd of
shoppers and idlers. Today, it was the opposite. I went to
Auchan in the middle of the afternoon, having worked
since morning on my book and feeling contented with
it. I went to fill the void—the rest of the day, in this case.
Or as a reward. To put myself in idle mode. Pure distraction. Maybe this is how I can come closest to feeling the pleasure others do in this place, that of young
people wandering about with no goal other than to buy
a pack of chips, or mothers who come by bus to spend
the afternoon, until it's time to pick the children up from
school, or anyone who comes here in the same way people used to go into town and *take a walk around* to see
what's going on.

On the second floor, a woman in her fifties approaches
me with a smile and a sort of timidity. "Are you Annie Ernaux?" I can't get used to the question. It's as if I needed
to assume a false identity while betraying nothing of the
deception. She has read a few of my books and wrote to
me fifteen years ago. She has just published an autobi-
ographical novel and *La Gazette du Val-d'Oise* wrote an
article about her. She is surprised to see me here. She
hates Auchan and almost never comes here. I tell her
that I come often and don't mind it. We part company on
her promise to send me a copy of her book.

I have to go down to Level 1 before I can recover my tranquility as an anonymous customer. I cross the bookstore area. On a little bench, barely visible behind a wall that separates it from a deserted information counter, a fashionably dressed young woman is immersed in a book whose title I cannot see. Next to her, a child is reading a comic book. I see to my delight that they are sitting just below the "reading prohibited" sign.

The prohibition is violated with complete serenity in the newspaper area, very well stocked, but *Le Monde* isn't sold there in the evening as it is at newsagents everywhere in Île-de-France, and will be available only in the morning. I leaf through various weeklies. A woman reads *Oulala!,* a young man *10 sport,* another *La Gazette des transferts,* and a young woman reads *People.* A man standing a little apart is absorbed in a science periodical. The rack of daily papers, *Le Parisien, Libé, Le Figaro, L'Équipe,* is almost empty at this time of day. Some magazine covers are creased. The *100 photos pour la liberté de la presse* brochure shows signs of repeated handling. Auchan is more concerned with unpaid candy at the super discount store than with damaged reading material.

It is a pleasant place, very quiet, almost secret, so hidden at the very back of the store, next to a scant gardening section. Gathering a community of readers.

THURSDAY, FEBRUARY 7

Half past four. Near the entrance to Auchan, two girls blew past me, one chubby, all dressed in gray, including her headscarf, the other slender with a black headscarf and black boots. I see them again in the health and beauty section, talking animatedly by the nail polish. Up until a certain age, girls never go by themselves to buy cosmetics or go to the bathroom.

At the checkout, a woman gathers her scanned items and puts them in plastic Auchan bags with a slow pace that one suspects is deliberate. She shows the cashier that one bag has just torn and asks for a replacement. The cashier tells her to go get another. She slips behind the customers in the line and returns unhurriedly. People watch her every movement in silence. Aware of the tension, the cashier helps the customer to transfer the items from the bag with the hole to the new one. The atmosphere of disapproval is palpable before this person who *takes her time* with no concern for that of others. Who flouts the implicit rules of consumer civility, of a code of conduct that alternates between rights—such as refusing an item that turns out to be defective, or double-checking one's receipt—and duties—not jumping the line at the checkout, always letting a pregnant or disabled person go ahead, being polite to the cashier, etc.

The fever pitch of movement that pervades large retail outlets drops sharply at the checkout. The line, a snare that cannot be escaped except at the risk of ending up in one far worse, renders us immobile. In the superstore aisles, people are *presences* that one passes and vaguely sees. Only at the checkout do they become individuals.

The checkout is the stage most susceptible to tension and irritation: with regard to the cashier, whose speed or slowness one hastens to assess; with regard to customers

whose shopping carts are overflowing (though no more than ours)

who have not noticed the absence of a barcode on an item, and will have to go back to the shelves to exchange it

who take a checkbook from their bag, heralding a series of ritual gestures—careful removal of the check, verification of the ID card and the writing of its number on the back of the check, the signing of the check, its surrender, goodbye and thank you—which seems intolerable, the final straw of waiting.

Wait time at the checkout is the time when we are closest to each other. Observed and observing, listened to and listening—or just getting a sense of each other in a drifting intuitive way.

Here, as nowhere else, our way of life and bank account are exposed. Your eating habits, most private interests, even your family structure. The goods deposited on the conveyor belt reveal whether a person lives alone, or with a partner, with a baby, young children, animals.

Your body and gestures, alertness or ineptitude, are exposed, as well as your status as a foreigner, if asking for a cashier's help in counting coins, and consideration for others, demonstrated by setting the divider behind your items in deference to the customer behind, and stacking your empty basket on top of the others.

But we don't really care about being exposed, in the sense that we do not notice and, most of the time, do not talk to each other. As if to strike up conversation would be absurd. Or simply unthinkable for some, with their look of being there but also not, to signal that they are a cut above the great majority of Auchan's clientele.

WEDNESDAY, FEBRUARY 13

3 p.m. No school today, so there are gangs of girls whose laughter travels from one section to the next. I notice that one girl, heavily made up, wears bright pink lipstick that matches her shoelaces.

In the seasonal promotions area, tables have been set up and children are drawing. The Year of the Snake began last Sunday and Auchan has not missed the event, offering a "Chinese Week" with special activities, the ideogram-writing, etc.

As I am choosing bags of food for my cats, a white-haired man addresses me:

"I have a six-month-old dog, can I give him canned food?"

"I don't have a dog but I think so. No, not those—" (the man is pointing to the boxes for senior dogs) "—he'll need the food for juniors."

I pull a package of four boxes from the shelf. He watches, puts the other ones back.

"Thanks very much. It's my grandchildren who wanted the dog. You get attached, eh!"

He smiles, walks next to me for a few steps, out of a simple desire to tell an unknown woman that he has a six-month-old dog, nothing more. I've noticed that, of all the departments, it is the one for animals that inspires the greatest yearning to talk.

In the checkout line, a woman with two children recognizes another who also has two children, and calls to her. The other exclaims, "Then we'll stay here, we won't go any further!" meaning they won't go to another cashier. The four children play together, the mothers chat and reminisce with excitement about Chinese New Year (they are not Asian). "At school, they ate Chinese food!" Is it the school that educates or is it the superstore? Maybe both.

A list in black ballpoint found in a shopping cart:

curly lettuce

flour

ham, lardons

grated cheese, yogurt

Nescafé

vinegar

I compared it with mine:

Ricoré coffee

lady fingers

mascarpone

milk, cream

sandwich bread

cat [canned food and kibble for]

post it notes

The superstore contains approximately fifty thousand food products. Considering that I must use a hundred of them, there remain 49,900 with which I am not familiar.

WEDNESDAY, FEBRUARY 20

Inside Auchan, traffic flows smoothly, with no congestion or collisions between shopping carts (I've noted that their "drivers," like those of cars, do not look at each other). Children pull wheeled baskets almost as big as they are.

In the frozen foods section, the Buitoni "meat supreme" pizza is on sale at 3.99€ . . . so the old one-cent-less trick that lowers the price to the unit below still works! It is possible that the superstore is selling off meat-based dishes in view of a recent case of horsemeat that was labeled beef, which is stirring public opinion.

The line I'm in ends up at two different checkouts. At some point, it's not a bad idea to choose between the two cashiers toiling away back to back, to make a subtle calculation based on the presumed speed of each cashier and the number of items in the cart of the customer ahead. Today, seeing the cashier on the left turning an item this way and that in her fingers and looking over the top of her glasses to type in the code, I place my bet on the other one, a young black woman with a black headband that nicely frames her forehead, though the cart of the customer ahead of me in that line is quite full. The lady, in her sixties, seems determined to arrange her shopping in a methodical fashion. She sets a packet of noodles on the conveyor belt, moves it, rummages around to place certain items in front of others. She blows out her breath several times, as if overcome by the difficulty of her task. Which fails: her articles are strewn over the entire length of the conveyor belt, making it impossible for me to put mine down. She takes out a big, sturdy, red plastic bag, shakes it vigorously to open it, and moves to the other side of the cashier to collect her purchases. She stuffs them into the bag with sudden dexterity, and pays by card. In her expression I discern relief at a mission accomplished. This is not the shopping cart of a woman who lives alone.

Superstores and supercenters continue to be extensions of the domain of women, of a domestic world that women keep in good working order by pacing through the aisles with mental lists of everything *missing* from the cupboards and the fridge, everything they need to buy to be able to answer the question "What are we going to eat tonight?" (or tomorrow, or all week). Women, more than men, possess the culinary skills that enable them to choose, without hesitation, grocery items according to the dish to be made, whereas a man, lost and defeated before a row of goods, will call for help, cell phone pressed to his ear: "Say, what kind of flour should I get?"

A dialogue heard on France Inter radio, a few years ago, between two male journalists in their thirties:

"My fridge is always full, my mom fills it for me!"

"Ha ha, yeah, isn't that always the way!"

They laughed with satisfaction. At having remained, in some way, infants.

THURSDAY, FEBRUARY 28

The dashboard of my car shows 3° outside. The pleasure of being enveloped by heat the moment you enter Door 2 of the shopping center. Walking around in a warm atmosphere wherever you go is almost like stepping off a plane in Cairo on arrival from Paris. Forget the mud, the cold, dreary weather, and the traffic. Slow down, abandon yourself to the warmth. Lose all sense of time—because there are no clocks, time is nowhere to be seen. Some girls are very lightly dressed. The children's winter jackets are removed and folded over the stroller. It is a summer's walk in winter.

A memory of my astonishment upon first entering the shopping center in the mid-1970s, wandering about, sheltered from the rain and cars, in clean, well-lit aisles where sound was muted, back then by wall-to-wall carpet. Going in and out of doorless boutiques, browsing at the Temps de Vivre bookshop, letting the children run around without fear. I felt a secret thrill to be at the very heart of hypermodernity, which, for me, the place symbolized in a fascinating way. It was like an existential promotion.

Today I watched people stroll by shop windows with barely a glance. Two women were sitting on the bench across from the escalator between C&A and an expensive boutique that sells Karl Lagerfeld. Isn't coming to the shopping center a way of being admitted to the spectacle of a party? Immersed, truly, not through a TV screen, in light and wealth, and worth as much as things. One may, in this place, feel disoriented and uneasy, but never *devalued*.

THURSDAY, MARCH 14

Ahead of me in line at the Auchan checkout is a woman whose face seems to be fixedly turned in the direction of the cashier. All I can see is the green and silver headscarf that descends from her hairline to her lower back. She does remove the items from her basket, but waits for those of the customer ahead to be scanned before placing hers on the conveyer belt. Only a bag of ten baguettes and several packets of Panzani pasta. Her gestures are not slow but almost imperceptibly delayed, hesitant. She opens a change purse, pulls out a banknote and some coins, which she puts down on the conveyer belt. The cashier counts the coins, asks for another, then one more. This takes some time. The woman leaves, carrying the heavy bag of baguettes. She hasn't said a word during the transaction. I thought, for her to go to Auchan alone, what an ordeal it must have been, one that even all her veils could not make bearable.

My turn comes. As usual, the cashier leans over to check if I have emptied the entire contents of my shopping cart onto the conveyor belt. Inside I've left *Le Monde,* which I did not buy at Auchan but at the news and tobacco shop in the shopping center. The cashier takes me to task. I tell her that I didn't buy the newspaper at Auchan, and, to justify myself, I add, not realizing how presumptuous it is of me to do so, that the issue is not yet available at Auchan and won't be until tomorrow morning. As if it were part of her job as cashier to check the date on *Le Monde*. She repeats that everything purchased outside the store must be wrapped in plastic at the entrance. "You understand, if your bags get checked, I'm the one who gets an earful. We get told off more and more, it's getting worse and worse."

I have just been put in my place for not having considered hers. Her "worse and worse" haunts me. Among the seven million working poor in France, many are cashiers.

In the language of mass distribution, the "prod" of a cashier is the number of items scanned per minute. Three thousand per hour is considered a good number.

MONDAY, MARCH 25

10 a.m. When the superstore is almost empty, as it is this morning, in the face of all the merchandise, one is overcome by a hallucinatory feeling of excess. The dead silence of goods as far as the eye can see. The customers seem to move slowly, as if overcome by lethargy, the kind exuded by the almost unreal vision of the cluttered

heap of food and objects. Or they're just people with time on their hands on Mondays—workers on their day off—or who have time all the time, retirees.

The shopping cart that I took at the entrance to Level 2 doesn't roll well. I realize that it is dented on one side; the chain used to attach it to other carts has been torn off. It is a cart that must have traveled out of the parking lot to help someone move house, or to play bumper cars, etc. It's amazing, all the things you can probably do with a shopping cart. I don't understand why they aren't borrowed more often. At one euro it's a bargain. I try more or less adeptly to get this one to work.

Surprise, the newspaper stand has migrated to Level 2, after household linens, near an entrance and a line of cash registers—a more visible location than before, also more exposed. It is now a kind of concourse, wide, brightly lit, with newspapers and magazines neatly arranged along two partitions facing each other. Nowhere to sit, not even on the piles of papers. Not a single nook or cranny. Everything seems designed to make the place inhospitable, to dissuade people from lingering, browsing, reading. And as a matter of fact, there is no one there.

Easter eggs galore. Already. I'd forgotten. Big retail stores don't forget anything. There are probably swimsuits in boxes waiting to be unpacked, like the gifts for Mother's Day. Commercial authorities abbreviate the future and consign last week's past to oblivion.

A guy in a coat, balding with glasses, is humming to himself, his little plastic bag in hand.

I realize that there is never any music inside of Auchan. Perhaps so as not to clash with that of the shopping center, barely noticeable. I find myself regretting the absence of music, songs that suddenly strike the memory and stir inexplicable joy, just as one is taking a pack of mineral water from a shelf. One time at Leclerc, it was Dalida, "Come prima."

WEDNESDAY, APRIL 3

On Level 1 of Auchan, in the seasonal promotions area, the Spring Wine Fair is on. Mostly single men. Behind the wines, another sales promotion: two perpendicular walls of women's shoes in flashy colors, green, red, pink, and, as in a living room, pouffes scattered here and there on which to sit and try on shoes at leisure. So far, the "invitation"—that must be the intention—has no takers.

On Level 2, the food level, it seems to me that the hanging yellow price signs have grown more and more glaring. Always the same equation, above the bins of

meat: pork at less than one euro per person. After checking, it seems that the said person is supposed to eat 110 g,
which, on the plate, after cooking and not including
waste, probably corresponds to 80 g. I quickly calculate:
a family of four who would eat this meager portion daily
would still spend 120€ per month. The superstore's art of
making people believe in its benevolence.

Dozens of bags of Easter eggs have been marked
down and tossed into bargain bins, a vaguely repugnant
mound that attracts no one. The party ended three days
ago.

A woman occupies the dairy aisle with a double
stroller facing outward: cute twins whose bright eyes
follow everyone.

At the checkout, where quite a few people are waiting, a customer with a wheeled shopping basket offers
me her spot. As I vigorously decline (do I look that tired?
that old?), she smiles and says she knows my writing. We
converse about the store, about the children, plentiful
on Wednesdays. Placing my items on the conveyer belt,
I think a little uneasily that she is going to look at what
I've bought. Every item suddenly takes on loaded meaning, reveals my lifestyle. A bottle of champagne, two bottles of wine, fresh milk and organic Emmental, crustless
sandwich bread, Sveltesse yogurt, kibble for spayed and
neutered cats, English ginger jam. It is my turn to be observed, I am an object.

FRIDAY, APRIL 5

Noon. Newsstand, Auchan. I cannot get used to places where magazines and newspapers are sold without a vendor to help you find what you're looking for. Unable to locate *La Quinzaine littéraire,* I take the previous evening's edition of *Le Monde.*

Nor is there anyone at the self-checkout, where a lost-looking girl is growing increasingly upset, not knowing where to put the items she takes from her basket, and driven to panic by the eyes that watch her every movement while the robot voice intones, over and over, "Place your items on the scale," as if it were dealing with a halfwit. Through a stunning reversal, it is the machines that look smart and humans stupid. I can't get used to this system, either. Now you can enter and leave a superstore the way you do an F1 Hotel,[6] without a word or a glance at others.

Nearly a third of checkouts are now automated, grouped by four or six and requiring no human presence except for that of one employee, who supervises and makes sure the machines are functioning correctly. During the day, there are only half as many traditional checkouts in use as automated checkouts. The extinction of cashiers presses on.

---

6. A French economy hotel brand owned by Accor. Opened in 1984 in France under the name Formule 1, it was renamed HotelF1 in 2007 and later rebranded as a roadtrip-themed hotel brand.

FRIDAY, APRIL 12

In an aisle, I pass a woman whose hair is concealed by a black veil from which a white band protrudes, similar to the wimple worn by of the nuns of my youth, the good sisters who incurred our mockery not so much because of their attire as because of their vow of perpetual chastity, which seemed insane to us—never to be with a man, how was it possible! Altogether different from the woman with the headscarf, who may well be devoted to God but also to a man (there is one standing next to her), which changes everything. Unless God and man are one. But there again, on the scale of pleasure, the Muslim woman with her headscarf still wins. And on the scale of freedom? But how to evaluate that? And how is it any of my business? Why does the question of their freedom torment me more than that of other women's freedom? In their place, I would be secretly proud of prompting so many questions, which, however, the media never gives them a chance to answer.

TUESDAY, APRIL 23

3:50 p.m. Young people have deserted the newspaper and magazine section. There's just a man standing in front of the well-stocked shelf of "Arrow-crossword" books and a woman seizing a copy of *60 millions de consommateurs.*

In the cleaning section, three young black men confer, heads together, over different brands of laundry detergent. I restrain the urge to advise them.

A woman, two little girls, a teenager, and an older woman, perhaps the grandmother, walk down the toilet paper aisle, in single file, purposefully, without a cart. The oldest girl, trailing behind, protests, "But it's such a big store!" Her comment surprises me. To feel a sense of ownership of a place means to no longer feel its size. Habit has erased from my mind the reality of Auchan's surface area (several thousand square meters), which, however, is recorded by my body. I prefer to give up on items that I forgot to get at the opposite end, rather than retrace my steps.

WEDNESDAY, APRIL 24

An eight-story building collapsed near Dhaka, Bangladesh. At least two hundred are thought to have died. Three thousand workers were employed in garment workshops there for Western brand names. To specify "Western" has long been redundant.

TUESDAY, APRIL 30

In front of the entrance to Auchan on Level 1, at the bottom of the big two-way *moving walkway,* is a space like a small waiting room, with seats in brown leather arranged back to back. They are rarely empty, often occupied in the morning by elderly North African men—Chibanis. Sitting there, one is free to watch the ballet of customers who come and go, and the security guard—a giant black man—pacing up and down the entire length of the checkouts. One can keep an eye out for possible incidents, in particular ones that arise as a result of the rule against entering with a backpack, or items purchased elsewhere, which are supposed to be sealed in transparent packaging with a temperamental guillotine-style device. As from a café terrace, though free of charge, one can watch the world go by and go about its business. *Lose oneself* in contemplation.

This afternoon, a man sits in a deep sleep in one of the seats, a forearm crutch lying on the armrest. Two women chitchat.

MONDAY, MAY 6

The feeling that some products are never bought, some sections never visited, even at other times of day.

Yet there is always traffic around the messy heaps of boxes that constitute a peculiar pharmacopoeia—*Orthosiphon,* royal jelly, marine collagen (?). A man stands, lost in thought. I read BURN FAT; ELIMINATE EXCESS WATER; PUT AN END TO UNWANTED KILOS. I imagine his body oozing water through every pore, shriveling to nothing. Well-positioned in the passage that connects the two wings of Level 2, the section is a complement to those that are overloaded with food; it treats the guilt of overeating.

At the end of my errands, I stop by the bookstore section to buy *Deux vies valent mieux qu'une* by Jean-Marc Roberts as a gift. I look for it, without getting my hopes up, in the display of bestsellers that fills ten feet with only ten titles, as if these were the only books you had to read and they were necessarily the best. There is Marc Levy, Françoise Bourdin, Laurent Baffie, Régine Deforges, and—surprise—a Roberts, but this one is an American whose first name is Nora. Nor do I see it among the books on the tables, a haphazard spread of novels, reportage, biographies. Some are shopworn. A man I hadn't noticed before, perhaps in charge of the section, hurries toward a kind of a lectern, looking busy, opens a register, writes something down. I have the feeling I'll disturb his calculations by asking for the book I haven't found. I feel sad and humiliated even before his ambiguous reply of no, we don't have it. As if I were looking for an item that has never existed.

In any case, I always feel bad placing a book on the conveyer belt, as if it were a sacrilege. Though I'd be happy to see one of mine pulled from a shopping cart and slid onto the belt between a pound of butter and a pair of tights.

FRIDAY, MAY 10

4:30 p.m. Mother's Day is everywhere in the shopping center. At Auchan, there's a dedicated space for it, filled with food processors, vacuum cleaners, coffee makers (apparently a must), perfume, etc.

It is the May school holiday period and the crowd is mostly women with shopping carts and children. I imagine the mighty line that all these mothers would form, scattered through the store with their carts and children, moored to subsistence and child-rearing. A prehistoric vision.

WEDNESDAY, MAY 15

The death count from the collapse of Rana Plaza in Bangladesh is 1,127. Found in the rubble were brand labels for Carrefour, Camaïeu, and Auchan.

THURSDAY, JUNE 27

The long banner strung over Door 2 of the shopping center reads SALES. Underneath is the smiling face of a woman in her thirties, in closeup, and behind her, smaller, a man's face, and a child's. Nothing has changed since Émile Zola's *The Ladies' Paradise;* women are always the primary—consenting?—targets of commerce.

To avoid the crush, I've chosen to do my grocery shopping at Auchan after all the other stores have closed, at 8 p.m. Still, traffic is heavy in the food and household-maintenance aisles, where the sales consist of offering products in giant quantities. A woman pushes a full shopping cart with several big packages of toilet paper standing one on top of another, fifty rolls at least. It is the inexorable logic of accumulation. The slogan from a very old TV commercial went: "*On a toujours besoin d'un petit pois chez soi,*"[7] a home always needs green peas. And a home always needs TP, shampoo, cooking oil, UHT milk, etc. Stories and films about famine are unbearable.

Surprise items for the next school year—and the superstore's goal is always to surprise—have popped up in the seasonal promotions area. A little girl sitting on the

7. The slogan for one of the first TV ads (for green peas), aired in 1968, echoing the famous verse of La Fontaine "On a toujours besoin d'un plus petit que soi," literally "We always need someone smaller than ourselves."

floor unfolds a map of the world. On Level 2, it is "Eastern Week," semolina, dates stuffed with almond paste, candied lemons, and sugar-powdered Turkish Delight, irresistible. I am transported back to longings from childhood and, for a few seconds, filled with rapture that such a place of abundance can exist.

WEDNESDAY, JULY 3

7:30 p.m. The back-to-school space is all set up now, ablaze with binders, pencil cases, notebooks, stationery, each more colorful than the next. A fairyland of school supplies that children of twenty years ago would have never dreamed of. BRING IN YOUR OLD SCHOOLBAG AND RECEIVE A CHECK FOR TEN EUROS, to be deducted—as one might expect—from the purchase of a new one. It is never too soon to inculcate the value of the new—which, as we know, is so nice until the novelty wears off, to the detriment of its use value. How to resist that promise of happiness, sporting a brand-new schoolbag on that distant first day back at school, a brand-new student on the brink of a brand-new year . . . but where do the old schoolbags go?

I look at the planners, the schoolchild's breviary, apparently in use as of first grade, or even kindergarten,

with covers that are dumbed-down—prehistoric animals, monsters, Spiderman, etc.—as well as sexist. A
Mickey Mouse questions the (male) notebook owner se-
verely, "Did you do your homework?" while Minnie flat-
ters his female counterpart, "You're the best!"

Leaving the section, I become aware of the strange
pleasure it gave me.

Tonight the wait in the checkout line is endless. I re-
sign myself to it. I sink into a kind of torpor where the
noise from deep inside the superstore at this peak hour
makes me think of the sound of the sea when one is doz-
ing on the sand.

THURSDAY, JULY 11

Mid-afternoon. On Level 2, I try to detach one of the
chained shopping carts by inserting a euro coin—nothing happens. I speak to the black security guard who
paces back and forth all day in front of the checkouts.
With an instrument he unlocks the recalcitrant trolley
and gestures at the next one in line, weary and impene-
trable. He returns to his surveillance of bags and racks
under strollers, with a bored nonchalance.

It is sheer chaos at the fruits and vegetables. The clang of carts colliding. Determined faces, arms and hands plunged into a heap of apricots, one euro per kilo, palpating and rejecting them, stuffing them in bags, in a joyous frenzy of gathering. The apricots are as hard as stones.

A few meters away, in the space set up for Ramadan, an ecstatic little boy holds a pack of dates stuffed with pink and green almond paste.

Indifferent to the xenophobic fears of one part of society, the superstore adapts to the cultural diversity of its clientele, scrupulously keeping pace with their holidays. No ethics are involved, just "ethnic marketing." Proponents of liberalism, however, would have an easy time extolling the virtues of this truly egalitarian and integrative function of the Market.

I see that a new form of headscarf has appeared, decorated with beads, hiding the hair while leaving the neck and nape uncovered. It reminds me of certain old-time headdresses from the provinces of France that we saw in pictures at school.

I wander around the non-food level among the swimsuits and underwear. I look up at the ceiling, for the first time—who ever does this in a superstore? Up above the neon lights that cast their dazzling rays on the world of merchandise below, I see a kind of casing inside of which, between the beams, there is a snarl of pipes and cables, and metal objects I cannot identify. They make up a forbidding, shadowy mass that contrasts with the general sparkle of the store. At this moment it occurs to me that my demeanor could appear suspect, as if I were looking for surveillance cameras. WE REMIND YOU THAT THIS SECTION IS MONITORED BY VIDEO SURVEILLANCE, I read as I walk by the stockings and pantyhose.

The fitting rooms of yore, discreet and managed by an employee, have disappeared and been replaced by three tiny nooks in a hollow in the wall, separated by just a curtain from the aisle where customers walk back and forth. There are no more saleswomen. Instead there is a warning: WE WISH TO INFORM OUR VALUED CUS-TOMERS THAT FITTING ROOMS MUST ONLY BE USED FOR TRYING ON CLOTHING (LIMIT 3 PER PERSON).

In plain speak (always translate superstore language), it is forbidden to sleep, eat, make love in the fitting rooms. For the moment, the curtain is open and a tired teenaged girl sits quietly chatting with her mother, who stands facing her.

Here, on another summer evening, I was stuck in a line so long that it stretched all the way to the cookie shelves, from which the checkout could not be seen. People did not speak to each other but peered ahead to assess how quickly the line was moving. It was very hot. A question came to me, one I often ask myself, the only one worth asking: why don't we revolt? Why not avenge ourselves for the wait imposed on us by the superstore, which reduces its costs by cutting back on staff, and all together decide to dig into the cookies and the chocolate bars, treat ourselves to free samples as a way of killing time in this wait to which we are condemned like rats trapped among shelves upon shelves of food, but more docile than rats, for we do not dare to nibble? To how many people does this thought occur? I cannot know. Had I taken the lead, no one would have followed me, as we know from the film *Le grand soir (Not Dead)*. We were all too tired, and soon we'd finally be outside, out of the snare, forgetful, almost happy. We are a community of desires, not of action.

My childhood dream, as a *war child* fed with stories of pillaging in 1940, was to freely enter deserted stores and take everything that struck my fancy—cakes, toys, school supplies. Whether or not one has lived it out, the dream may still be somewhere in the superstore, vague and drifting. Bridled, repressed. There are no more shop windows to protect the sardines of the Prévert poem, the famous "Grasse matinée." There's no more need of them. Canned food, steaks, galettes Saint-Michel, and strawberry Tagada, all of which one can touch and take in one's hands, but never put in one's mouth, are much better protected by this system of incessantly monitored freedom, by internalized fear.

At the "no-purchase exit," the security guard eyes one's hands and pockets. As if to leave without merchandise were an anomaly that rendered one suspect. Guilty *de facto* for not buying anything.

WEDNESDAY, JULY 17

Inside the shopping center, the shops are closed. The background music is more audible than in the middle of the day, when it is drowned out by a loud humming noise. All life has fled to the immediate vicinity of Auchan. I realize I have never seen it closed, never seen the metal barriers pulled down—or drawn—in front of the checkouts. No one sees them, except for the security guards, since it is the first business in the center to open and the last to close. The McDonald's, Flunch, and bowling alley all have access to the outside.

Again my feet take me to the books. In the "Romance" section I am amused, in a manner of speaking, to note the staying power of a vernacular that has been around for a century: THE BRIDES OF SUMMER, FIANCÉE FOR ONE NIGHT, DREAMS OF A BRIDE, AN ARRANGED MEETING.

There is a plethora of cookbooks. I flip through the one by Ginette Mathiot, from which I once learned how to feed others more than just spaghetti and yogurt cups. It's a new edition, modified quite a bit. On the cover is a photo of a young brown-haired woman in a T-shirt in her kitchen. In her right hand she holds a whisk and in the other, Ginette Mathiot's book, which she reads with the smile of one absorbed in an uproarious novel. The perennial woman surrounded by pots and pans. I walk away, unsettled. Maybe I have come to Auchan tonight to see my twenty-five-year-old self.

I remark to the young black cashier that he is astonishingly quick. He is pleased. This is not, as I'd thought, a summer job for him. He exclaims: "I've worked at Auchan for four years!"

"I come here often but I've never seen you . . . "

"That's not surprising, I usually work in the aisles. I unpack boxes and put things on the shelves."

"Which do you prefer, the cash register or the aisles?"

He says the aisles are harder. It hurts your back bending down all the time.

The sun has set. People are sitting at outdoor tables at McDonald's, facing the half-empty garage where the cars drive faster than in the daytime. I take the ramp that connects the lower garage with the one at the top, open to the sky. With the lights turned off behind the mirrored windows, the compact mass of the shopping center seems covered in black mica.

MONDAY, SEPTEMBER 30

Now, at the entrance to Level 1 at Auchan, there are dozens of little devices, all the same, slotted into a rack in parallel rows. One might almost think they were big phones or remote controls. They are neither. These are scanners that customers may use to scan items themselves. The amount is displayed as things are added. Final payment is made at one of the *Rapid* checkouts on Level 2. No need to remove items from the cart. This is self-scanning. A little white sign specifies the main term of use: the possession of an Auchan loyalty card. Fickle consumers, be gone! A lecture follows for the others, full of praise for time and effort saved but also veiled threats. The scanner-user is warned that A PIECE OF ID must be presented on payment. A *re-scan* of one's shopping and *random checks* may be performed.

Right away I imagine the scene. One or two supervisors appear. "Hello. May I ask you to empty your cart?"

"Why?"

"To check if you have really paid for everything."

I wonder what the questioning will be based on—what external signs, picked up by the cameras. And whether the shopping-cart bouncers will do their business on the spot, in front of other customers, or take you away, and if so, where. Going through the checkout will become more perilous than clearing Customs.

On the internet I read that the scanning device is called a gun, and that consumers claim to be satisfied with the system, with the weapon that eliminates cashiers while at the same time turning us over to the discretionary authority of the superstore.

A simple political act: refuse to use it.

To avoid all temptation (I know the insidious coercion of mass distribution, and my own weakness as a consumer), I cut up my Auchan card.

TUESDAY, OCTOBER 22

I stopped writing in my journal.

As I do every time I cease to record the present, I feel I am withdrawing from the movement of the world, giving up not only narrating my days, but seeing them too. Because seeing in order to write is to see in a different way. It means to *distinguish* objects, individuals, and mechanisms, and to give their existence value.

As the months went by, I was able to measure the controlling force exerted by mass production spaces in real and imaginary ways. By provoking desires at dictated times, its violence equally present in the colorful profusion of yogurt flavors as in the gray everyday deals aisles, and by reinforcing social stigmas through the *accommodation* of individuals with low incomes. The items purchased, whether in a little heap or a toppling mountain on the conveyor belt, are nearly always among the cheapest. Upon leaving the superstore, I was often overwhelmed by a sense of helplessness and injustice. But for all that, I have not ceased to feel the appeal of the place and the community life, subtle and specific, that exists there. It may be that this life will disappear with the proliferation of individualist sales schemes such as online ordering and curbside pickup, apparently gaining ground each day among the middle and upper classes. So today's children, in adulthood, may remember with nostalgia Saturday shopping at the Hyper U, as those of over fifty remember the pungent grocers' shops of the past where they went with a metal pitcher to get fresh milk.

ANNIE ERNAUX (b. 1940) is the winner of the 2022 Nobel Prize in Literature and the author of over twenty published works. Her books have won numerous awards in France and internationally, including the Prix Renaudot in 1984, the Marguerite Duras Prize, 2008, the Strega Europeo Prize in 2016, and, in 2017, the Marguerite Yourcenar Prize for her body of work. In 2018 Ernaux won the Premio Hemingway; in 2019, she won the Prix Formentor; and in 2021, she was elected a Royal Society of Literature International Writer. She holds an honorary doctorate from the University of Cergy-Pontoise.

ALISON L. STRAYER is an award-winning writer and translator. Her work has been shortlisted twice for the Governor General's Award for Literature and for Translation. She has also been shortlisted for the Grand Prix du Livre de Montréal. Her translation of Annie Ernaux's *The Years* was shortlisted for the Man Booker International Prize in 2019 and won the 2018 French-American Translation Prize in the nonfiction category as well as the Warwick Prize for Women in Translation, honoring both author and translator.